Praying through Grief

Praying through Grief

POEMS AND MEDITATIONS FOR HEALING

COMPILED BY
KATE KIRKPATRICK

LION

Compiled by Kate Kirkpatrick
This edition copyright © 2010 Lion Hudson
The author asserts the moral right
to be identified as the author of this work

A Lion Book
an imprint of
Lion Hudson plc
Wilkinson House, Jordan Hill Road,
Oxford OX2 8DR, England
www.lionhudson.com
ISBN 978 0 7459 5510 0

Distributed by:
UK: Marston Book Services, PO Box 269, Abingdon, Oxon, OX14 4YN
USA: Trafalgar Square Publishing, 814 N. Franklin Street, Chicago, IL 60610
USA Christian Market: Kregel Publications, PO Box 2607, Grand Rapids, MI 49501
First edition 2010
10 9 8 7 6 5 4 3 2 1 0

Acknowledgments
Scripture quotations taken from the "Holy Bible, New International Version", copyright
© 1973, 1978, 1984 International Bible Society. Used by permission of Zondervan and
Hodder & Stoughton Limited. All rights reserved. The "NIV" and "New International
Version" trademarks are registered in the United States Patent and Trademark Office
by International Bible Society. Use of either trademark requires the permission of
International Bible Society. UK trademark number 1448790. p. 24: Extract from the
"Authorized Version of the Bible" (The King James Bible), the rights in which are
vested in the Crown, are reproduced by permission of the Crown's Patentee, Cambridge
University Press. p. 11: Excerpt taken from *Through Grief*, by Elizabeth Collick, published
and copyright 1986 by Darton Longman and Todd Ltd, London, and used with the
permission of the publishers. p. 32: "When I see your empty chair" © 2010 Kate
Kirkpatrick; p. 52: Extracts from *Common Worship: Pastoral Services* are copyright © The
Archbishops' Council and are reproduced by permission. p. 62: Extract from *Motherhood
and God*, by Margaret Hebblethwaite, reproduced by kind permission of Continuum
International Publishing Group. p. 79: "Let us so bind ourselves" prayer is excerpted from
The Way of the Cross, written and illustrated by Caryll Houselander, © 2002 by Liguori
Publications, www.liguori.org. Used by permission.

A catalogue record for this book is available
from the British Library
Typeset in Bembo
Printed and bound in China

Contents

Introduction

This book is a companion for the grieving. Though death comes to us all, its inevitability cannot fully prepare us for the pain of losing a loved one. The path through grief is slow and often circuitous; it is rarely free of setbacks. But it has been travelled before, and the wisdom of those who have preceded us can ease our pain:

Give sorrow words: the grief that does not speak
Whispers the o'er-fraught heart, and bids it break.

Shakespeare, *Macbeth*, IV.3

This collection includes words of desperation and words of healing. Some may be comforted by Henry Scott Holland's oft-quoted "Death is nothing at all"; others will not. But my hope is that in this book you will discover, if not a mirror of all of your feelings, a sufficiently true reflection to help you find your way through grief.

1

A Time to Grieve

Between grief and nothing I will take grief.

William Faulkner

So like fear

What's wrong with the world, to make it so flat, shabby, worn-out looking? […] No one told me that grief felt so like fear. I am not afraid, but the sensation is like being afraid. The same fluttering in the stomach, the same restlessness… At other times it feels like being mildly drunk, or concussed. There is a sort of invisible blanket between the world and me.

C. S. Lewis

Escaping grief

Only the unloved
and unloving
escape grief.

Claire Rayner

A time for everything

There is a time for everything,
   and a season for every activity under
      heaven:
a time to be born and a time to die,
   a time to plant and a time to uproot,
a time to kill and a time to heal,
   a time to tear down and a time to build,
a time to weep and a time to laugh,
   a time to mourn and a time to dance,

a time to scatter stones and a time to

    gather them,

  a time to embrace and a time to refrain,

a time to search and a time to give up,

  a time to keep and a time to throw away,

a time to tear and a time to mend,

  a time to be silent and a time to speak,

a time to love and a time to hate,

  a time for war and a time for peace.

Ecclesiastes 3:1−8

Why?

Why should a dog, a horse,
  a rat have life,
And thou no breath at all?

Shakespeare, *King Lear***, V.3**

Give us strength

Support us, Lord, when we are silent through grief!
Comfort us when we are bent down with sorrow!
Help us as we bear the weight of our loss! Lord, our
Rock and our Redeemer, give us strength!

Jewish prayer

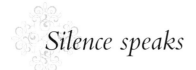

Silence speaks

The day you bury him is a day of chores and crowds, of hands false or true to be shaken, of the immediate cares of mourning. The dead friend will not really die until tomorrow, when silence is round you again.

Antoine de Saint-Exupéry

From day to day

When you're bereaved you're so all over the place that you might find a book heartwarming on a Tuesday and mindless nonsense on a Wednesday.

Virginia Ironside

Out of the depths

Out of the depths I cry to you, O Lord;

O Lord, hear my voice.
  Let your ears be attentive
  to my cry for mercy.

Psalm 130: 1–2

Care draws on care, woe comforts
  woe again,
Sorrow breeds sorrow, one grief brings
  forth twain.

Michael Drayton

Life and Death

The two old, simple problems ever
  intertwined,
Close home, elusive, present, baffled,
  grappled.
By each successive age insoluble, pass'd on,
To ours to-day — and we pass on the same.

Walt Whitman

The Reaper and the Flowers

There is a Reaper, whose name is Death,
   And, with his sickle keen,
He reaps the bearded grain at a breath,
   And the flowers that grow between.

"Shall I have naught that is fair?" Saith he;
   "Having naught but the bearded grain?
Though the breath of these flowers is sweet to me,
   I will give them all back again."

He gazed at the flowers with tearful eye,
   He kissed their drooping leaves;
It was for the Lord of Paradise
   He bound them in his sheaves.

"My Lord has need of these flowerets gay,"
         The Reaper said, and smiled:

"Dear tokens of the earth are they,
  Where he was once a child."

"They shall all bloom in fields of light,
  Transplanted by my care,
And saints, upon their garments white,
  These sacred blossoms wear."

And the mother gave, in tears and pain,
  The flowers she most did love:
She knew she should find them all again
  In the fields of light above.

O, not in cruelty, not in wrath,
  The Reaper came that day;
'Twas an angel visited the green earth,
  And took the flowers away.

Henry Wadsworth Longfellow

2

The Valley of the Shadow of Death

I wake and feel the fell of dark, not day.

Gerard Manley Hopkins

He restoreth my soul

The Lord is my shepherd; I shall not want. He maketh me to lie down in green pastures: he leadeth me beside the still waters. He restoreth my soul: he leadeth me in the paths of righteousness for his name's sake. Yea, though I walk through the valley of the shadow of death, I will fear no evil: for thou art with me; thy rod and thy staff they comfort me. Thou preparest a table before me in the presence of mine enemies: thou anointest my head with oil; my cup runneth over. Surely goodness and mercy shall follow me all the days of my life: and I will dwell in the house of the Lord for ever.

Psalm 23

An Element of Blank

Pain—has an Element of Blank—
It cannot recollect
When it began—or if there were
A time when it was not—

Emily Dickinson

As you walk

Do not hurry as you walk with grief,
It does not help the journey.
Walk slowly, pausing often:
Do not hurry as you walk with grief.

Be not disturbed
By memories that come unbidden.
Swiftly forgive;
And let Christ speak for you unspoken words.
Unfinished conversation will be resolved in Him.
Be not disturbed.
Be gentle with the one who walks with grief,
If it is you, be gentle with yourself.
Swiftly forgive;
Walk slowly, pausing often:
Take time.
Be gentle as you walk with grief.

Celtic prayer

Watch and soothe us

Watch, dear Lord,
with those who wake,
or watch, or weep tonight
and give your angels
charge over those who sleep;
tend your sick ones,
bless your dying ones,
soothe your suffering ones,
pity your afflicted ones,
shield your joyous ones,
and all for your love's sake.

St Augustine of Hippo

In your everlasting arms

Lord, in weakness or in strength
we bear your image.
We pray for those we love
who now live in a land of shadows,
where the light of memory is dimmed,
where the familiar lies unknown,
where the beloved become as strangers.
Hold them in your everlasting arms,
and grant to those who care
a strength to serve,
a patience to persevere,
a love to last
and a peace that passes human understanding.
Hold us in your everlasting arms,
today and for all eternity;
through Jesus Christ our Lord.

Christian prayer for mourning

An ancient path

Those who are worn out and crushed by this mourning, let your hearts consider this:
this is the path that has existed from the time of creation and will exist forever.
Many have drunk from it and many will yet drink.
As was the first meal, so shall be the last.
May the master of comfort comfort you.
Blessed are those who comfort the mourners.

Jewish blessing

A Better Resurrection

I have no wit, no words, no tears;
  My heart within me like a stone
Is numbed too much for hopes or fears.
  Look right, look left, I dwell alone;
I lift mine eyes, but dimmed with grief
  No everlasting hills I see;
My life is in the fallen leaf:
  O Jesus quicken me.

My life is like a faded leaf,
  My harvest dwindled to a husk:
Truly my life is void and brief
  And tedious in the barren dusk;
My life is like a frozen thing,
  No bud or greenness can I see;
Yet rise it shall – the sap of Spring;
  O Jesus rise in me.

My life is like a broken bowl,
   A broken bowl that cannot hold
One drop of water for my soul
   Or cordial in the searching cold;
Cast in the fire the perished thing;
   Melt and remould it, till it be
A royal cup for Him, my King:
   O Jesus drink of me.

Christina Rossetti

Without you

When I see your empty chair
I am hollow;
What is left of me, without you?

When silence sounds your absence
I am deafened;
What is left of me, without you?

Take my emptiness
Make it full;
Take my silence
Make it speak;
Take my lack and make it
Overflowing thanks
For the good that has been;
And help me see
That more can be.

Kate Kirkpatrick

Darkness impenentrable

Bereavement is a darkness
impenetrable to the imagination
of the unbereaved.

Iris Murdoch

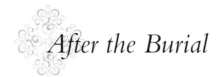

After the Burial

Your logic, my friend, is perfect,
Your moral most drearily true;
But, since the earth clashed on her coffin,
I keep hearing that, and not you.

James Russell Lowell

Christ be with me

Christ be with me, Christ within me,
Christ behind me, Christ before me,
Christ beside me, Christ to win me,
Christ to comfort and restore me,
Christ beneath me, Christ above me,
Christ in quiet, Christ in danger,
Christ in hearts of all that love me,
Christ in mouth of friend and stranger.

St Patrick's Breastplate

Come unto Me

Come unto Me, the Master says: –
  But how? I am not good;

No thankful song my heart will raise,
  Nor even wish it could.

I am not sorry for the past,
  Nor able not to sin;

The weary strife would ever last
  If once I should begin!

Hast thou no burden then to bear?
  No action to repent?

Is all around so very fair?
  Is thy heart quite content?

Hast thou no sickness in thy soul?
  No labour to endure?

Then go in peace, for thou art whole;
   Thou needest not his cure.

Ah, mock me not! I often sigh;
   I have a nameless grief,

A faint sad pain – but such that I
   Can look for no relief.

Come, come to him who made thy heart:
   Come weary and oppressed;

To come to Jesus is thy part,
   His part to give thee rest.

New grief, new hope he will bestow,
   Thy grief and pain to quell;

Into thy heart himself will go,
   And that will make thee well.

George MacDonald

3

Give Sorrow Words

Ever has it been that love
knows not its own depth
until the hour of separation.

Kahlil Gibran

I measure every grief I meet

I measure every grief I meet
With analytic eyes;
I wonder if it weighs like mine,
Or has an easier size.

I wonder if they bore it long,
Or did it just begin?
I could not tell the date of mine,
It feels so old a pain.

I wonder if it hurts to live,
And if they have to try,
And whether, could they choose between,
They would not rather die.

I wonder if when years have piled—
Some thousands—on the cause
Of early hurt, if such a lapse
Could give them any pause;

Or would they go on aching still
Through centuries above,

Enlightened to a larger pain
By contrast with the love.

The grieved are many, I am told;
The reason deeper lies,—
Death is but one and comes but once
And only nails the eyes.

There's grief of want, and grief of cold,—
A sort they call "despair",
There's banishment from native eyes,
In sight of native air.

And though I may not guess the kind
Correctly yet to me
A piercing comfort it affords
In passing Calvary,

To note the fashions of the cross
Of those that stand alone
Still fascinated to presume
That some are like my own.

Emily Dickinson

The power of tears

There is a sacredness in tears.
They are not the mark of weakness,
but of power.
They speak more eloquently
than 10,000 tongues.
They are the messengers
of overwhelming grief,
of deep contrition,
and of unspeakable love.

Washington Irving

# Farewell

Farewell to Thee! But not farewell
To all my fondest thoughts of Thee;
Within my heart they still shall dwell
And they shall cheer and comfort me.

Life seems more sweet that Thou didst live
And men more true that Thou wert one;
Nothing is lost that Thou didst give,
Nothing destroyed that Thou hast done.

Anne Brontë

Prayer for the departed

O God, give him rest with the devout
   and the just
in the place where green things grow
   and refreshment is and water
the delightful garden,
   where pain and grief and sighing
   are unknown.

Egyptian epitaph

My heart

Write Your blessed name, O Lord, upon my heart,
there to remain so indelibly engraved,
that no prosperity,
no adversity shall ever move me from Your love.
Be to me a strong tower of defence,
a comforter in tribulation,
a deliverer in distress,
a very present help in trouble and a guide to heaven
through the many temptations and dangers of this life.
Amen.

Thomas à Kempis

Valleys and trenches

Grief is like a long valley, a winding valley where any bend may reveal a totally new landscape… Sometimes… you are presented with exactly the same sort of country you thought you had left behind miles ago. That is when you wonder whether the valley isn't a circular trench.

C. S. Lewis

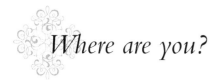

Where are you?

Over a number of years the artist K. Kollwitz worked on a monument for her younger son who was killed in October 1914. His death became for her a sort of personal obligation. Two years later she noted in her diary:

There's a drawing made, a mother letting her dead son slide into her arms. I could do a hundred similar drawings but still can't seem to come any closer to him. I'm still searching for him as if it were in the very work itself that I had to find him.

Catalogue of an exhibition of the works of K. Kollwitz, London 1967

The weight of sorrow

It is natural, in sorrow, to be consoled if a friend shares our grief. First, sorrow weighs one down; it is a load which, of course, one tries to lighten. When therefore a person sees others joining him in sorrow, it feels as if they are helping him carry the load, trying to lessen its weight on him; so the burden weighs on him less heavily, just as in the case of carrying physical weights.

St Thomas Aquinas

The pang of change

There is something in the pang of change
More than the heart can bear
Unhappiness remembering unhappiness.

Euripides

Ring Out, Wild Bells

Ring out, wild bells, to the wild sky,
The flying cloud, the frosty light;
The year is dying in the night;
Ring out, wild bells, and let him die.

Ring out the old, ring in the new,
Ring, happy bells, across the snow:
The year is going, let him go;
Ring out the false, ring in the true.

Ring out the grief that saps the mind,
For those that here we see no more,
Ring out the feud of rich and poor,
Ring in redress to all mankind.

Ring out the want, the care the sin,
The faithless coldness of the times;

Ring out, ring out my mournful rhymes,
But ring the fuller minstrel in.

Ring out false pride in place and blood,
The civic slander and the spite;
Ring in the love of truth and right,
Ring in the common love of good.

Ring out old shapes of foul disease,
Ring out the narrowing lust of gold;
Ring out the thousand wars of old,
Ring in the thousand years of peace.

Ring in the valiant man and free,
The larger heart, the kindlier hand;
Ring out the darkness of the land,
Ring in the Christ that is to be.

Alfred, Lord Tennyson

Give us hope

O God, who brought us to birth,
and in whose arms we die,
in our grief and shock
contain and comfort us;
embrace us with your love,
give us hope in our confusion
and grace to let go into new life;
through Jesus Christ.

Book of Common Worship

What never dies

They that love beyond the world
cannot be separated by it.
Death cannot kill what never dies.

William Penn

4

Love Immortal

Life is eternal; and love is immortal; and
death is only a horizon; and a horizon is
nothing save the limit of our sight.

Rossiter W. Raymond

The difference one makes

Sometimes, when one person is missing, the whole world seems depopulated.

Lamartine

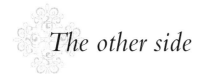

The other side

D*eath hides –*
But it cannot divide,
Thou art but on
Christ's other side.
Thou with Christ
And Christ with me
And so together
Still are we.

Author unknown

Why do you weep?

When you are sorrowful look into your heart and you shall see that you are weeping for that which has been your delight.

Kahlil Gibran

Come back

You tell me "she goes on".
But my heart and body are crying out,
come back, come back.

C. S. Lewis

Miss Me, But Let Me Go

When I come to the end of the road,
and the sun has set for me.
I want no rites in a gloom-filled room.
Why cry for a soul set free?
Miss me a little but not too long,
and not with your head bowed low.
Remember the love that was once shared.
Miss me, but let me go.

For this is a journey we all must take,

and each must go alone.

It's all a part of the master's plan,

a step on the road to home.

When you are lonely and sick of heart,

go to the friends we know.

Bear your sorrow in good deeds.

Miss me, but let me go.

Author unknown

Incomprehensible love

Sometimes God's love seems incomprehensible. I have two friends whose babies have died, one at ten weeks, the other at one week. Those babies who died were real persons, as their mothers knew they were. To all eternity they will exist as human persons, and yet what kind of eternity can we imagine for them? We cannot imagine. We cannot envision how God can bring to fruition in eternity the personality lost to this world. What did they achieve in this world? Only a message of the existence of love, a love whose size can be measured by the size of the pain that it leaves behind.

Margaret Hebblethwaite

Requiem

When I am dead, my dearest,
  Sing no sad songs for me:
Plant thou no roses at my head,
  Nor shady cypress tree:
Be the green grass above me
  With showers and dewdrops wet;
And if thou wilt, remember,
  And if thou wilt, forget.

I shall not see the shadows,
  I shall not feel the rain;
I shall not hear the nightingale
  Sing on, as if in pain;
And dreaming through the twilight
  That doth not rise nor set,
Haply I may remember,
  And haply may forget.

Christina Rossetti

Do not stand at my grave and weep

Do not stand at my grave and weep;
I am not there. I do not sleep.
I am a thousand winds that blow.
I am the diamond glints on snow.
I am the sunlight on ripened grain.
I am the gentle autumn rain.
When you awaken in the morning's hush
I am the swift uplifting rush
Of quiet birds in circled flight.
I am the soft stars that shine at night.
Do not stand at my grave and cry;
I am not there. I did not die.

Mary Elizabeth Frye

The heart's memory

The heart hath its own memory, like the mind.
And in it are enshrined the precious keepsakes,
into which is wrought the giver's loving thought.

Henry Wadsworth Longfellow

What is Death?

Death is nothing at all
I have only slipped away into the next room
I am I and you are you
Whatever we were to each other
That we are still

Call me by my old familiar name
Speak to me in the easy way you always used
Put no difference in your tone
Wear no forced air of solemnity or sorrow

Laugh as we always laughed
At the little jokes we always enjoyed together
Play, smile, think of me, pray for me
Let my name be ever the household word that it always was
Let it be spoken without effort

Without the ghost of a shadow in it

Life means all that it ever meant
It is the same that it ever was
There is absolutely unbroken continuity

What is death but a negligible accident?
Why should I be out of mind
Because I am out of sight?

I am waiting for you for an interval
Somewhere very near
Just around the corner

All is well
Nothing is past; nothing is lost
One brief moment and all will be as it was before
How we shall laugh at the trouble of parting when
*   we meet again!*

Henry Scott Holland

When I am gone away

Remember me when I am gone away,
  Gone far away into the silent land;
  When you can no more hold me by the hand,
Nor I half turn to go yet turning stay.
Remember me when no more day by day
  You tell me of our future that you plann'd:
  Only remember me: you understand
It will be late to counsel then or pray.
Yet if you should forget me for a while
  And afterwards remember, do not grieve:
  For if the darkness and corruption leave
  A vestige of the thoughts that once I had,
Better by far you should forget and smile
  Than you should remember and be sad.

Christina Rossetti

The most I ever did for you

The most I ever did for you
was to outlive you.
But that is much.

Edna St Vincent Millay

Crossing the Bar

Sunset and evening star,
And one clear call for me!
And may there be no moaning of the bar,
When I put out to sea,
But such a tide as moving seems asleep,
Too full for sound and foam,
When that which drew from out the boundless deep
Turns again home.

Twilight and evening bell,
And after that the dark!
And may there be no sadness or farewell,
When I embark;

For tho' from out our bourne of Time and Place
The flood may bear me far,
I hope to see my Pilot face to face
When I have crost the bar.

Alfred, Lord Tennyson

5

Comfort and Consolation

Peace, peace! he is not dead, he doth not sleep –
he hath awakened from the dream of life – 'Tis we,
who lost in stormy visions, keep with phantoms an
unprofitable strife.

Percy Bysshe Shelley

Turn Again to Life

If I should die and leave you here a while,
be not like others sore undone,
who keep long vigil by the silent dust.
For my sake turn again to life and smile,
nerving thy heart and trembling hand
to do something to comfort other hearts than thine.
Complete these dear unfinished tasks of mine
and I perchance may therein comfort you.

Mary Lee Hall

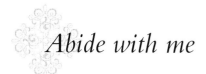

Abide with me

Abide with me;
Fast falls the eventide;
The darkness deepens;
Lord, with me abide;

When other helpers fail,
And other comforts flee,
Help of the helpless,
O abide with me.

Henry Francis Lyte

Gone from my sight

I am standing on the sea shore,
A ship sails in the morning breeze and starts for the ocean.
She is an object of beauty and I stand watching her
Till at last she fades on the horizon and someone at my
side says:
"She is gone."

Gone! Where?
Gone from my sight – that is all.
She is just as large in the masts, hull and spars as she was
when I saw her
And just as able to bear her load of living freight to its
destination.
The diminished size and total loss of sight is in me,
not in her.

And just at the moment when someone at my side says,
"She is gone",
There are others who are watching her coming, and other
voices take up a glad shout:
"There she comes"
– and that is dying. An horizon and just the limit of our
sight.
Lift us up, Oh Lord, that we may see further.

Bishop Brent

The purest heaven

May I reach
That purest heaven, be to other souls
The cup of strength in some great agony,
Enkindle generous ardour, feed pure love,
Be the sweet presence of a good diffused,
And in the diffusion ever more intense!
So shall I join the choir invisible
Whose music is the gladness of the world.

George Eliot

Let us so bind ourselves

Let us so bind ourselves
that we will not only
adhere to You
in times of consolation,
in times of sweetness and devotion
and when life goes smoothly,
but yet more securely
in the bleak and the bitter
seasons of the soul—
in the hard iron of the winters
of the spirit.

Caryll Houselander

When sorrow walked with me

I walked a mile with Pleasure.
She chattered all the way,
But left me none the wiser
For all she had to say.
I walked a mile with Sorrow,
And ne'er a word said she;
But oh, the things
I learned from her
When Sorrow walked with me!

Robert Browning

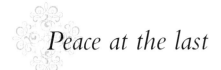

Peace at the last

O Lord, support us all the day long,
   until the shadows lengthen and the evening comes,
   and the busy world is hushed,
   and the fever of life is over,
   and our work is done.

Then in your mercy grant us
   a safe lodging,
   and a holy rest,
   and peace at the last.

John Henry Newman

God be in me

God be in my head,
and in my understanding;
God be in my eyes,
and in my looking;
God be in my mouth,
and in my speaking;
God be in my heart,
and in my thinking;
God be at my end,
and at my departing.

Sarum Primer

Understanding backwards

Life can only be understood backwards;
but it must be lived forwards.

Søren Kierkegaard

Where does my help come from?

I lift up my eyes to the hills –
　　where does my help come from?

My help comes from the Lord,
　　the Maker of heaven and earth.

He will not let your foot slip –
　　he who watches over you will not slumber;

indeed, he who watches over Israel
　　will neither slumber nor sleep.

The Lord watches over you –
　　the Lord is your shade at your right hand;

the sun will not harm you by day,
  nor the moon by night.

The Lord will keep you from all harm –
  he will watch over your life;

the Lord will watch over your coming and going
  both now and forevermore.

Psalm 121

Make me an instrument

Lord, make me an instrument of your peace,
were there is hatred, let me sow love;
where there is injury, pardon;
where there is doubt, faith;
where there is despair, hope;
where there is darkness, light;
where there is sadness, joy.

O Divine Master, grant that I may not so much seek to be
consoled as to console;
to be understood as to understand;
to be loved as to love.

For it is in giving that we receive;
it is in pardoning that we are pardoned;
and it is in dying that we are born to eternal life.

St Francis of Assisi

The secret of death

You would know the secret of death.
But how shall you find it unless you
seek it in the heart of life?

Kahlil Gibran

Depth nor height can part

Unfathomed love divine,
Reign thou within my heart;
From thee nor depth nor height,
Nor life nor death can part;
My life is hid in God with thee,
Now and through all eternity.

George Wallace Briggs

Index of first lines

Index of authors